LIVE, LAUGH, BURN IT DOWN (and Rebuild Something Better)

A Soul Reclamation Manifesto for the Burned Out, Brilliant, and Ready for More

DEDICATION

To my family—my everything.

To my beautiful girls, Allie, Chloe, and Liz:
You inspire me every single day. You make this world the most beautiful place.

To my husband, Alex:
The supporter of dreams. The man who showed me what unconditional love looks like when I had no idea how to even recognize it. I adore you.

Table of Contents

Before We Live, Laugh, and Burn It Down - A Permission Slip, A Pep Talk, and a Friendly Warning: This Book Might Change You.

This is not a book you read. It's one you remember yourself through.
I wrote this for the part of you that's tired of playing small—
not because you're broken,
but because you're waking up.

Be honest:
Have you ever looked around and thought,
"Is this seriously the best we could do?"

A world where billionaires race to the edge of space for a ten-minute selfie,
where politicians argue like drunk uncles at Thanksgiving,
where your grocery bill feels like a personal attack —
and somehow, you're supposed to stay "positive" and "productive" through it all.

You're not crazy for feeling it.
You're not broken.
You're not failing at life because you're tired, frustrated, or secretly dreaming of moving to a cabin with zero Wi-Fi.

You're awake.

And the truth is — the old world is coming undone.
Not because you're lazy.
Not because people "just don't work hard enough."
But because it was built on the wrong foundation from the

beginning:
fear, greed, division, control.

You didn't come to Earth to audition for your own life.
You didn't come here to hustle for the right to exist.
You are worthy because you are.

If you've ever laughed at the absurdity, cried at the heaviness, or
stood outside at night wondering why it all feels so off—

Good.

It means you're ready.

The world you were born into is ending.
The world you were born for is beginning.

And it needs you wide awake, fiercely alive, and unshakably free.

Ashes are not the end. Ashes are where the new fire begins.

CHAPTER 1

The Death of the Old World (And Why It's Good News)

If you're reading this, it's because you can feel it, can't you?

The world isn't ending.
It's shedding its skin.

When you see chaos, maybe — just maybe — it's not destruction.
Maybe it's transition.
Maybe it's the old world breaking open to make room for something more honest, more alive.

What feels like loss right now — like we feel in this country, like you might feel in your own life — it's not failure.
It's liberation.
Liberation from everything that tethered you to systems that were never built to love you.
Never built to nourish you.
Never built to see the breathtaking soul that you are.

The systems that once told you how to live, who to be, what to fear — they are dying.
Not because you failed them.
But because they failed you.

And you, beautiful soul —
You're not here to patch up the broken walls of a crumbling world.

You're here to build something new.
You're here to be the midwife to a future that's already crowning
— wild, raw, breathtaking.
There's no time for waiting rooms or second-guessing.
The world is asking you to catch it with your bare hands.

The falling apart you see around you?
It's not tragedy.

It's a long-overdue clearing.
It's fierce mercy —
the kind your heart has been quietly praying for, even when you
didn't have the words.

For too long, the old world ran on fear:
Fear of not being enough.
Fear of forever struggling, of giving everything and still feeling
unseen.
Fear of speaking your truth and losing love.
Fear of hoping for more and being called foolish for it.
Fear of the brilliant, stubborn light inside of you —
the part that refused to give up even when everything around you
said, "Settle."

You were taught to believe that the noise outside mattered more
than the knowing inside.
You were taught that belonging meant shrinking.
That success meant forgetting who you are.

But let me ask you something:

Have you ever — even in your loneliest or most exhausted
moments — felt that flicker deep inside that whispered,
"There has to be more than this..."
Even when you didn't know what "more" looked like?

That voice is real, my friend.

It's the oldest part of you.
The part they tried to bury under obligations and expectations
and exhaustion.
The part that never gave up on you.

And the beautiful news?
That voice will always answer when you call it home.

As the old-world cracks and crumbles —
as the soil turns dry and the trees hollow out —
you might feel a grief you can't quite explain.

It's okay.

Grieve.

Grief is holy.
Grief means you loved.
You loved the dream of a world that could have been gentler.
You loved the hope that life could be simple, safe, beautiful.

Honor that love.
Honor that grief.

But don't lose yourself inside it.

Because the story isn't ending here.

Take a breath, and dare to wonder:

What if something even more beautiful is trying to be born through me?

The smoke you see rising isn't just destruction.
It's the clearing of the fields.

Its sacred space being made —

For new dreams,

For truer ways of living,

For more honest ways of being.

Can you feel it — even if it's just the tiniest flicker?
Can you feel the part of you that never quite fit into the old
world — stretching its wings, remembering how to fly?

The old institutions — governments, media, big corporations, outdated
education systems — are crumbling.

And not because they were strong.

They're falling apart because, underneath all the fancy titles and official logos,
they were hollow all along.

They told us they had the answers.
They told us they knew better.
They told us if we just played along — worked hard enough,
stayed quiet enough, waited patiently enough — they would take
care of us.

Spoiler alert:
They didn't.

They weren't building a better world for us.
They were building a bigger cage — with shinier bars.

And now, the walls are cracking.
The glitter is peeling off.
The promises are falling flat.

Because no system built on fear, control, and pretending ever stands forever.

And here's the best part:

Hearts are shifting.
Minds are stretching.
Dreams are starting to breathe again.

All around you, people are waking up —
longing for a world where they're free to love without limits,
to create without permission,
to dream without ridicule,
to be everything they are — and still be enough even when
they're doing absolutely nothing at all.

And maybe — just maybe — your heart has been stirring too.

Do you feel it?
That little tightening in your chest?
That warm ache you can't quite explain?

That's not anxiety.
That's awakening.

It's the first stretch of a soul that's been sleeping too long.
It's the first crack in the shell, the first reach for the light without
even knowing how.

There will be people who cling harder to the wreckage —
desperate to duct-tape the old world back together.
There will be people who shout louder, throwing fear like
confetti, hoping you'll get scared enough to sit back down.

Let them.

Let them cling.
Let them shout.

You?

You're not here to go back to sleep.

You're here to create.

You're here to remember the part of you that existed long before fear had a name.

You weren't made to survive a broken world.
You were made to build a better one.

So, take heart, brave soul.

You are not standing in the ruins of a failed world.
You are standing at the doorstep of a brand new one.

The Phoenix does not mourn the ashes.

The Phoenix rises because of them.

And you —
you are already rising.

If you ever feel overwhelmed by the noise of collapse, place your hand over your heart and remember:

You were never here to rescue broken systems.

You were always here to rise, to rebuild, and to remember who you truly are.

CHAPTER 2

Sovereignty Over Victimhood (Your Life Is Yours Again)

Let's be real.

You've been lied to.
About who you are.
About what you deserve.
About how small you're supposed to stay.

They made growing up sound like freedom —
and then handed you bills, deadlines, and a checklist of ways you
were supposed to prove your worth.

Maybe you thought there would be some grand moment —
a letter in the mail,
a tap on the shoulder,
Ed McMahon showing up at your door with a giant check,
or a mysterious lawyer announcing you had a secret, wealthy
uncle who left you his entire fortune.

Something. Anything.
Some sign that said,
"Congratulations — you're free now!"

But that letter never came.
The knock never came.
The fortune never came.

And if you're honest — part of you kept waiting anyway.

But here's the real plot twist nobody told you:

You're free now.
You always were.

The door?
It's been open the whole damn time.

No one's coming to hand you permission to live.
No one's coming to rescue you from your own life.

It's you.
It's always been you.

And this — right now — is the moment you get to walk out of the old story
they wrote for you.

Not just walk —
Dance. (Do the Harlem Shake, the Dougie.)
Run. (Skip. Ride away on your Jazzie scooter like you own the
road.)
Laugh.
Create.
Be.

You're not here to survive a system that never loved you.

You're here to remember you were never trapped to begin with.

Now listen —
I know "sovereignty" sounds like one of those words you hear on a History
Channel documentary at 2AM.

It sounds fancy.
Maybe even a little intimidating.
But it's actually so simple a six-year-old could teach it to you.

Sovereignty just means:
You belong to yourself.

That's it.

Your mind.
Your heart.
Your choices.
Your life.

All yours.

Not your boss's.
Not the government's.
Not your parents'.
Not your partner's.
Not that random stranger on Facebook.
Not the person on TikTok who didn't like your makeup review.
Not even the guy at the gas station who side-eyed your snack choices.

Yours.

But it can't lead you where your soul wants to go now.

You can't build the life you're aching for by hiding in the ruins of the old one.

Which, speaking of...

Knock knock.
Who's there?

Sovereignty.
Sovereignty who?

Uhm... didn't we just go over this a few paragraphs back??

You know — the whole "you belong to yourself" spiel?
The "your mind, your heart, your choices, your life" stuff??
but PAY ATTENTION.

Because Sovereignty isn't just a word.

It's the whole key to everything you came here to remember.

It's the freedom you thought someone else had to give you —
but that was always sitting quietly inside you, like a birthday
present you forgot to open.

Or like that random Amazon package you forgot you ordered,
and when it shows up, it's somehow exactly what you needed at
exactly the right moment.

Or like that crockpot meal you set and forgot about —
and a few hours later you're walking around your house thinking,
"What smells so good?"
and realize,
"Oh right — it was me. I did that. I just forgot how good it could
be."

That's what sovereignty feels like.

It's not always loud.

Sometimes it's just a flicker.
A scent.
A whisper.
A forgotten gift inside you, waking up and saying,
"Hey... you belong to yourself."

And it smells delicious, my friend.

Sovereignty means you don't have to wait for someone else's approval to exist fully anymore.

You don't have to wait for a committee to vote on your dreams.
You don't have to shrink yourself to make other people comfortable.
You don't have to apologize for wanting more — or less — or different.

You get to be the damn CEO of your own soul.

Now, I'm not saying it's always easy.

When you've spent your whole life thinking someone else holds the keys to your freedom,
it can feel a little terrifying to realize...

you were the locksmith all along.

Especially when life keeps throwing curveballs —
like your favorite TV show killing off your favorite character,
which causes you to spiral for days and tear up every time you hear Hozier singing Work Song.

(I'm looking at you, 9-1-1. *I'll never forgive you for taking Bobby Nash from the world —especially by exposure to a super-strain of Crimean-Congo hemorrhagic fever.* Really? THAT'S how you did him dirty?)

Because grief is real.
Loss is real.

Shock is real.
Even when it comes wearing a firefighter's uniform on primetime TV.

And sometimes — let's be honest —
it just feels easier to blame the writers, the politicians, the
economy, your boss, the universe itself —
anyone but yourself —
because if they're in charge, at least it's not your fault when life
feels unfair.

But deep down... you already know.

You know who's been holding the pen to your own story this whole time.

You.

And look — I get it.

Victimhood?
It has its perks.

When the world feels unfair, it's way easier to throw your hands
up and say,
"Well, what can you do? Life's just like that,"
and go back to binge-watching a show where, at least this time,
maybe your favorite character won't die of some absurd virus no
one had ever heard of before.

(No promises, though. TV writers are savages.)

But deep down...
you know you're not actually helpless.
You never were.

Victimhood was a survival skill.
It was armor.

It was a way to make sense of a broken world when you were too tired, too hurt, or too overwhelmed to fight for yourself.

And you know what?
It worked.
It got you here.

It protected you when you needed protecting.

But it can't lead you where your soul wants to go now.

Because sovereignty isn't always a lightning bolt.
It isn't always a "throw down your apron and storm dramatically out of Applebee's" moment.
(Although if you feel called, I fully support that journey.)

Most of the time, sovereignty shows up quietly.
Almost sneakily.

It shows up like this:

You say "No thanks" to a group text that drains your will to live.

You close your laptop at exactly 5:00 PM without an ounce of guilt, like the badass CEO of your own time you secretly are.

You don't fold your laundry tonight —
you curl up instead to the sweet lullaby of Nate the Hoof Guy, carving away hoof rot, slapping a salicylic acid wrap on there to save the day — and somehow, it soothes your weary soul.

You take a break from life's chaos and watch S&B Pressure Washing videos, secretly wishing Spencer could pressure wash all the nonsense from your brain the way he obliterates grime from driveways.

You eat the damn cookie without giving it a TED Talk in your head about calories, guilt, and societal expectations.

You realize — maybe for the first time — you don't owe anyone an explanation for why you like what you like, believe what you believe, or live how you live.

That?

That's sovereignty.

Tiny rebellions.
Quiet revolutions.
Small moments where you whisper,
"I belong to me."

And the more you notice them,
the more they multiply.

The more you feed them,
the louder they sing.

Until one day,
you're not flickering anymore —
you're on fire.

And you're setting the world ablaze —
not in destruction —
but in new life.

You waiting for a gold-embossed invitation to live your damn life?

You think Amazon's gonna overnight you your freedom in a cute box with a Prime sticker on it?

Nope.

You already have it.

It's been sitting inside you this whole time —
like a crockpot meal you forgot you started,
quietly cooking,
filling the whole house with something warm and good
you almost forgot was yours.

It's ready.

YOU are ready.

(In my best Colonel Jessup voice — full courtroom meltdown
now:)

"SOVEREIGNTY?!
Son, we live in a world that runs on approval — and that
approval has to be guarded by people with NO backbone.
Who's gonna stand up for your freedom to say 'Nah, I'm good'?
You?
You, Lieutenant People-Pleaser?
You, Captain Postpone-Your-Own-Dreams?
You can't handle the truth —
which is that you're already free, and always have been!"

And okay, sure —
Colonel Jessup's about to be court-martialed, but...
he made a valid point.

Because what he was really trying to say —
in a slightly less yelly, definitely more emotionally intelligent way
—

is this:

You never needed their permission.
You never needed their map.

You were born with a compass inside you.
And that compass?
It still points true.

The world will always ask you to shrink.
I won't order a Code Red on you.

Because guess what?

It's up to you.

You have to choose it.
You have to choose you.

You belong to yourself.

Always have.
Always will.

"Every time you choose yourself, you teach the world how to treat you."

Let that sit in the silence.
Let it echo.
Let it become their new standard.

CHAPTER 3

Exiting the Fear Matrix: How to Stop Feeding What You Don't Want

You ever notice how fear has excellent production value?

The news has theme music.
Disaster updates come with sound effects and scrolling banners.
social media gives fear a stage, a spotlight, a "like" button, and ten thousand opinions you didn't ask for.

Fear knows how to put on a show.

It doesn't whisper.
It doesn't knock gently.
It kicks in the door, hijacks the playlist, and eats the last cookie.

And for most of us?
It worked.

Fear kept us quiet.
Fear kept us compliant.
Fear told us,
"Don't make waves. Don't ask for too much. Don't trust your own gut — we'll tell you what's safe."

And because we wanted to survive?
We listened.

Of course, we did.

Fear knows how to sound like safety when you're exhausted.

But here's the truth nobody profitable wants you to realize:

Fear only works when it's fed.

It needs your attention.
It needs your clicks.
It needs your panic.
It needs you to keep believing that the worst-case scenario is the most responsible one.

But what happens —
what happens when you stop feeding it?

What happens when you stop handing your energy to the voices shouting "What if everything goes wrong?"
…and start listening to the quieter question beneath it:

"But what if it goes right?

Sometimes fear doesn't show up like a monster.

Sometimes it shows up like a mortgage.
A spreadsheet.
A parent's voice in your head.
An Excel document titled "Realistic Life Goals."

And sometimes?

It shows up in HomeGoods on a wooden sign that says Live, Love, Laugh.

What does that even mean?

Is that the Rae Dunn of life mottos?
Do I need everything labeled with a sign to have permission to do it?

"Here's your tray labeled EAT. Your mug labeled COFFEE.
Your decorative bowl labeled JOY."
What's next — a throw pillow that says "BREATHE, BUT
ONLY IF YOU'VE EARNED IT"?

Let's be honest:

If I need to be told to "Live" ... maybe we're missing the bigger problem.

Fear loves this stuff.

It loves selling you pre-approved inspiration,
packaged nicely in beige and bold fonts,
as long as you never actually act on it.

Fear wants you to keep dreaming, but not doing.
Keep scrolling, but not choosing.
Keep organizing your life, but not living it.

Because if fear can keep you "inspired" but inactive —
it wins.

Let's be honest —
fear is sneaky.

It doesn't always scream.
It doesn't always wear black cloaks and shout doomsday prophecies.

Sometimes it slips into your daily habits like background noise.

Here's how you might still be feeding it without realizing:

Signs You're Still Feeding Fear: "Time to Ozempic that sucker out of your system"

You keep doomscrolling but call it "staying informed."

You over-research every possible outcome instead of making one tiny move forward.

You binge organizing videos instead of organizing your own life.

You ask 14 people what they think before you even trust yourself.

You hold off on doing something until you "feel ready" (spoiler alert: fear never thinks you're ready).

You watch motivational content like its church... but don't actually act on it.

You wait for the "perfect time" like it's a mythical creature that will appear in your living room.

You shrink your dreams until they fit neatly under the label "reasonable."

You pretend you're being "realistic," but what you're really being is afraid.

Starving Fear: Let That MLM Crumble

...But guess what?

We're about to starve that mother sucker.

We're giving fear a full dose of energetic Ozempic.

No more snacks.
No more attention.
No more letting it run your calendar, your choices, or your mind.

Let its voice hollow out.
Let its grip shrink down to nothing.
Let it waste away while you rise.

Because here's the thing:

Fear is a hustler.

It can run circles around all the Boss Babes.
It doesn't even need to send you a Facebook DM that says:
"Hey girl, haven't talked to you in forever! Hope you're doing great. Have you heard about [insert pyramid-shaped disappointment here]?"

Unlike that high school friend who just tried to Boss Babe her way into your life with essential oils and desperation,
Fear doesn't need a pitch.

It already knows you.

It knows your soft spots.
It knows your doubts.
It knows exactly how to dress up like "responsibility" and "realism"
so you'll keep giving it space on your vision board —
right next to the dreams it's trying to keep small.

But not anymore.

Because you're done letting fear pitch you your own limitations.

You're not buying.

Not today.
Not ever again.

How to Starve Fear (Without Burning Your Life Down in the Process)

You don't need to quit your job, sell your stuff, or go on a silent retreat in the desert to reclaim your freedom.
(Unless you want to. In which case, I fully support your Britney-shaving-her-head moment. Bring snacks.)

Starving fear doesn't require a dramatic plot twist.
It just requires consistency.

It requires catching the fear before you feed it.

It means not giving it dessert.

Here's how to start:

Simple, Sneaky Ways to Starve Fear:

Don't answer the guilt text. Even if it ends with "love you 🩶."
Especially then.
Love your damn self...
and don't respond.

Do one thing before you're ready.
Not ten. Not all. Just one.
Send the email. Buy the domain. Say the thing.

Let people misunderstand you.
Fear thrives on over-explaining.
It tells you to clarify, justify, tone it down.
But let them think what they want.

You're not a customer service rep for your soul.
Channel your inner Wendy's social media team.
Let. Them. Cook.

Because if they're gonna talk,
they might as well talk about something delicious.

Rest without justification.
No, you don't have to "earn it."
You don't need a migraine or a meltdown to deserve a nap.

Call joy "productive."
Because it is.
Joy recalibrates your entire vibration. Fear hates that.
Spin around in circles singing:
♫ "Goooooood, what have you done? ♩
You're a pink pony girl, ♫and you dance at the club—
♫Oh mama, I'm just having fun— ♫
On the stage in my heels, ♩
♫It's where I belong—
DOWN AT THE PINK PONY CLUB!!" ♫

Because maybe that's exactly what healing looks like sometimes.
Messy, sparkly, alive, and none of fear's damn business.

Set one boundary without apologizing.
Fear dies a little every time you say "no" with your whole chest and zero
guilt.

Turn down the volume on panic content.
Unfollow. Mute. Take back your attention.
Fear can't survive without airtime.

Speak your truth even if your voice shakes.
Fear will try to convince you that silence is safer.
But silence is where fear multiplies.

Stop treating worst-case scenarios like sacred prophecies.

Just because fear imagines it doesn't mean its truth.
Play the What If game — but flip it.
What if the opposite of your fear actually happens?
What if it does work out?
What if you're more than capable?
What if you're finally supported?
What if it's better than you imagined?

Suddenly, the spiral loses power.

You're not circling the drain anymore —
you're circling possibility.

And fear?
Fear can't breathe where hope is expanding.

These aren't massive acts.

They're tiny moments of rebellion
where you tell fear:
"Nah, I'm good."

And every time you do it —
you remember a little more of who you are.

Not who fear told you to be.
Not who the world rewarded you for being.
But who you actually are underneath all of it:

Free.

Exiting the Fear Matrix

You don't defeat fear by fighting it.
You starve it.
You ignore its DMs.
You mute its commentary.
You dance in your joy while it sulks in the corner.
You give it its weekly dose of 15mg Mounjaro and tell it to go lay
down.

Every time you choose delight over dread,
truth over performance,
rest over proving,
you are slipping one foot further out of the matrix.

You're not here to make fear comfortable.
You're here to remember:
You belong to yourself.
And you were never meant to live your freedom on a delay.

Fear wants you to be digestible. But you're the whole damn meal
and you season your food.

— "Be yourself; everyone else is already taken." — Oscar Wilde

CHAPTER 4

Currency of the Future: Community, Creativity, Contribution

"If productivity were currency, most of us would be millionaires — and somehow still bankrupt."

Let's be honest:
The old system taught you to measure your worth in how much you can produce, how fast you can go, and how well you can perform exhaustion like it's a personality trait.

But here's the thing:
You were never meant to be an economic machine with a Pinterest morning routine and chronic burnout.

You were meant to be a radiant, soul-powered being
who knows that value isn't just what you do — it's what you bring.

In the new world, the currency isn't hustle.
It's energy. Creativity. Connection. Presence.

And none of those can be found in a spreadsheet.
(Well, unless you're into really sexy spreadsheet design, in which case, I see you.)

The world told you that money was everything.

But the future?
The real future?

It runs on contribution, not consumption.
It runs on creativity, not conformity.
It runs on relationships, not reputation.
It runs on energy, not effort.

Because when you're aligned,
you don't have to hustle.
You flow.
You exchange.
You show up fully, and that alone has value.

Currency of the Future: Community, Creativity, Contribution

You've been taught to chase what looks valuable.

Degrees.
Promotions.
Brand deals.
Validation from people you wouldn't even trust to dog-sit.

But in the future, we're building?
We don't chase.
We exchange.

And the new currencies are things you've had all along —
You just weren't taught to see them as sacred.

Let's redefine the vault:

Presence is currency.
That moment when you truly see someone — or yourself —
without the filter, without the performance?
That's wealth.

Creativity is currency.
Not just paintings and poetry (though we love those).
But solutions. Possibility. Daydreaming.
You're literally printing abundance with your imagination.

Community is currency.
That phone call that makes you laugh-snort.
That ride-or-die group text thread.
That neighbor who waters your plants and brings you soup.
This is your social savings account.

Kindness is currency.
A compliment to a stranger. A deep breath instead of a snarky
clapback.
Every small grace deposit into the world you want to live in.

Rest is currency.
You being whole is more valuable than you being productive.
Read that again.

The old world sold your energy for scraps.

It said,
"Work harder and we might give you just enough to survive."

But I'm here now —
and I've got the black briefcase.

I'm meeting you in a public location,
hiding in plain sight like we're in some low-budget spy thriller.
(You know you've always wanted to do a black briefcase deal like
in the movies.
Don't lie.)

Granted, this isn't some Pulp Fiction situation —
no weird glowing mystery contents here.

No.

After our very secretive meet-up (preferably at a train station or
an eerily empty city park),
I'm going to crack open this briefcase,
and show you exactly what's inside:

The New World.

The new world says:

"Value yourself first — and watch everything rise to meet you."

No more bargaining for your worth.
No more exhausting yourself for scraps.
No more asking permission to live abundantly — in soul, in
spirit, in joy.

How to Trade and Spend Your Energy in the New World

Now that you've opened the briefcase,
seen the glint of the new world inside,
and realized you are already holding the new currency —
the question becomes:

Where will you spend it?

Because everything you do from here isn't just a task.
It's an investment.
It's a trade.
It's a soul exchange.

And just like you wouldn't walk into a pawn shop with a bag of diamonds and trade them for a Snickers bar and a broken remote control, you don't get to spend your energy like it's cheap anymore.

Welcome to Your New Economy:

Every moment you invest in your creativity?
You're generating wealth.

Every time you nurture a true relationship instead of a fake one?
You're growing equity.

Every breath you take without guilt?
You're stacking interest in your own expansion.

How to Start Trading Differently:

Before you give your time, ask: "Is this a soul deposit or a soul withdrawal?"
(If it's draining you like a leaky faucet, rethink the investment.)

Before you say yes, ask: "Am I saying yes to honor me — or to avoid guilt?"
(Hint: Fear loves guilt; your future loves boundaries.)

Before you sacrifice rest, ask: "Am I building, or am I bleeding?"
(Building feels alive. Bleeding feels resentful.)

Before you share your gifts, ask: "Am I planting seeds or throwing pearls at pigs?"
(Sometimes you're not unappreciated — you're just overwatering plastic plants.)

New Rule of the New World:

If it costs you your peace,
your energy,
your authenticity —
it's too damn expensive.

And I don't care how shiny it looks.

You can't afford to spend yourself cheap anymore.
You are no longer on clearance.
You are not a bargain bin of brilliance waiting for someone with a coupon.

You are the briefcase.
You carry the new world inside you.

Act accordingly.

What Happens When You Invest Sacredly?

When you start spending your energy like it's sacred —
everything changes.

You stop throwing your brilliance into black holes.
You stop trading your peace for approval.
You stop treating your life like a clearance rack.

Instead?

You start making compound interest deposits into your own future.

You start building soul equity that no market crash can touch.

You start creating wealth that no thief, no inflation, no crumbling empire can ever take away.

Because sacred investment?
It always multiplies.

Real Returns on Soul Investment

The right people start finding you.
Not because you chase — because your energy becomes a lighthouse they can't miss.
(No frantic networking. No "circle back on Q3 deliverables." Just energy that says: "Come correct or don't come at all.")

Opportunities open that hustle could never create.
Synchronicities replace strategies.
Magic replaces manipulation.
(Take that, Caleb Hammer. Sometimes the best return on investment isn't cutting Netflix — it's cutting the dead energy you've been entertaining.)

Peace stops being a vacation.
It becomes your baseline —
Your currency —
Your flex.
(Tell Dave Ramsey you've got a different kind of emergency fund now: it's called "My nervous system stays regulated even when things get weird.")

You start getting paid in ways money can't measure.
In belly laughs —
In true friendships —
In creative flow.

In mornings where you wake up and your chest feels lighter instead of heavier.

(No more budgeting your joy on a Dave Ramsey envelope system. Your currency is infinite — and you're spending it wildly, freely, intentionally.)

Look — I'm not telling you to blow your 401k and flee to Tulum.

(Unless you want to. In which case: send postcards, bring snacks, and good luck dodging all the digital nomad bros selling drop-shipping courses.)

But seriously —
value yourself like your future depends on it.

Because it does.

Giving Without Depletion / Receiving Without

When you start investing your energy sacredly,
you naturally start giving differently too.

You don't give because you're afraid.
You don't give because you're obligated.
You don't give because you're trying to buy love, approval, or a cosmic gold star.

You give because you're overflowing.

You give because you have it to give.

You give because your joy, your creativity, your presence isn't limited resources — they're self-replenishing wells.

Giving from Overflow (not Depletion):

You're no longer writing emotional checks you can't cash.
You're investing small, potent acts of presence — without draining your account.

You know… like when you're doing the laundry and find a $20 bill in the dryer.
You have no idea where it came from — maybe the universe, maybe your husband —
either way, it's yours now,
and it showed up just when you needed it...
smelling like Downy scent beads and divine timing.

That's how sacred presence works, too.
It adds up quietly in the background —
then shows up right on time, feeling like a little miracle.

You're not cosigning other people's emergencies out of guilt.
You're offering real support — but only when it honors you, too.

You're giving from a place of joy, not performance.
No more martyrdom-as-a-love-language energy.
(You're not bleeding for validation anymore — you're blooming from wholeness.)

Receiving Without Guilt:

Here's the wild part:

When you start honoring your soul's currency —
you naturally start receiving more.

Opportunities.
Connections.
Support.
Resources.
Magic.

It flows in because you finally believe you deserve it.

And when it arrives?
You don't apologize for it.
You don't shrink.
You don't make yourself small, so nobody feels uncomfortable
about your glow.

You say:
"Thank you. More please."

And then —
you order everything on your damn pretzel like Michael Scott.

You don't ask for "just one topping" or "whatever's included."
You order that sweet pretzel with the works —
all 18 available toppings:

Sweet glaze, cinnamon sugar, chocolate, white chocolate, fudge,
M&Ms, caramel dip, mint chip, chocolate chip, marshmallows,
nuts, toffee nuts, coconut, peanut butter drizzle, Oreo, sprinkles,
cotton candy bits, and powdered sugar.
ALL OF IT.

Why?
Because you can.
Because you're allowed to have joy in every flavor.
Because this isn't about "deserving" anymore —
it's about remembering.

You don't have to earn what already belongs to you.
You don't have to prove you're worthy of sweetness.

The new world doesn't ask you to shrink.

It invites you to rise.
To receive.
To savor.

So, leave this chapter with powdered sugar dust on your lips,
the sweet taste of Oreos still melting on your tongue,
and the unshakable knowing in your bones:

You're allowed to have it all.
Not because you performed.
But because you remembered who you are.

"You miss 100% of the shots you don't take. – Wayne Gretzky"
– Michael Scott

CHAPTER 5

Thriving in Chaos: Turning Instability into Opportunity

"The goal isn't to avoid chaos.
The goal is to become the version of you that knows what to do when it comes."

Let's be real:
The world still feels upside-down half the time.

Banks collapsing.
Prices soaring.
Systems glitching.
People arguing on the internet like they're being paid in rage coins.

Some days it feels like we're one group text away from collapse.

But here's what no one tells you:

Chaos isn't just destruction.
It's data.
It's design.
It's divine direction.

If you're still trying to wait for things to "settle down" before you live, create, or expand —
you'll be waiting forever.

Because we're not going back to "normal."
We're moving forward into what's true.

And thriving in chaos isn't about pretending you're not overwhelmed.
It's about learning to find the rhythm inside the storm.

Thriving in Chaos: Turning Instability into Opportunity

Bruce Nolan here, aboard the Maid of the Mist in fabulous Niagara Falls, New York.

First off:
The chaos didn't come to punish you.
It came to wake you up.
To what's not working.
To what's never been real.
To who you really are when nothing's performing for you anymore.

And yes — Bruce is about to have a meltdown of biblical proportions mid-news report,
so let's not get distracted by...
might I say... more chaos.

Because yeah — life might look like a tornado.
Your to-do list might be crying.
Society is glitching like an iPhone with 2% battery and 14 open apps.

But here's what they never taught you in school:

Chaos isn't the opposite of creation —
it's the birthplace of it.

And if you're here, reading this?
That means you're not just trying to survive the storm.

You're learning how to speak to the lightning.
How to listen to the cracks.
How to catch the pieces flying around you and turn them into blueprints.

What Chaos Really Is (And What It Isn't)

We've been taught to treat chaos like failure.
As if the mess means you messed up.
As if instability means you're unworthy of peace.
As if confusion = wrong path.

But what if we've had it backwards?

What if chaos is sacred friction — not because something's ending, but because something's out of alignment?
What if chaos isn't your punishment, but your pattern interrupter?

Sometimes things don't fall apart because you're broken.
They fall apart because you've outgrown the box, they were trying to keep you in.
That relationship?
That job?
That "safe plan" that suddenly makes you feel like you're suffocating?

It's not failing.
It's making space.

Chaos as Data, Not Doom

Chaos is full of messages, if you know how to listen.

It says:
"This structure can't hold your expansion."
"This belief no longer fits who you are."
"This version of you deserves a softer story."

It's the energetic equivalent of your favorite jeans ripping in public —
embarrassing, inconvenient, but also maybe the moment you realize you need to stop squeezing yourself into something that never fit in the first place.

Truth bomb:

Chaos doesn't ask for perfection.
It demands presence.

You don't have to know what happens next.
You don't need a step-by-step reinvention manual.
You just need to show up.
Soberly. Honestly. Even messily.

Because when you meet chaos with consciousness —
you start to compost the breakdown into breakthroughs.

Recognizing Your Survival Patterns

You can't thrive if you don't know what's been running the show.
And for most of us?

It hasn't been clarity.
It's been survival.

And hey — I'm sorry to do this to you…
but we're about to hit those survival patterns you've been using
to hold it all together.

So, you might want to strap in.

You remember in Twister?
That scene when the F5 tornado turns toward them —
Bill and Jo run to the pump house, tie themselves to the deepest
pipes in the ground, and ride out the most powerful storm of
their lives?

That's you right now.

But just like them?
You'll survive.

And like them, you're not just surviving for the sake of it —
you're about to watch Dorothy fly.

And she's going to record all the data points
about the patterns that have been ruling your life —
so you can get your own early warning system.

So, you can stop spiraling in storms you didn't even know you were still
dancing with.

So, you can take back control — not through gripping tighter,
but through knowing yourself more clearly than ever before.

Anchoring in Truth During the Storm

The world might still be spinning.
People might still be panicking.

Your group chat might still be a vortex of spiraling energy, bad memes, and low-vibe advice.

But you?

You're learning how to stand in the center of the storm without getting swept into someone else's fear forecast.

Because here's the deal:

Chaos doesn't mean you're unsafe.
It means your old anchors are being tested.

Real Anchors in Chaos Aren't "Control"

Trying to control everything around you in a storm?
That's not anchoring.
That's exhausting.

You don't need to predict every gust of wind.
You need to know what grounds you.

And that starts with truth.

Not generic self-help truth.
Not "what your aunt from Facebook thinks" truth.
Not algorithm-approved trending truth.

Your truth.
The one that vibrates in your belly and hums in your bones.

In the storm, your truth might sound like:

"I feel overwhelmed right now, and I can still be okay."

"I don't have to fix everything — just breathe through the next minute."

"This isn't personal. This is just the system glitching while I evolve."

"I'm allowed to pause. That doesn't mean I'm failing."

These aren't affirmations for the fridge.
These are anchors.

They tie you to the deepest pipe in the earth —
so when fear starts flailing, you don't get dragged with it.

Alchemizing the Mess: Turning Instability into Growth

Here's the secret they don't teach in the burnout Olympics:

Your chaos holds ingredients for your next evolution.
The wreckage isn't just there to be mourned.
It's there to be mined.

That's not toxic positivity.
That's spiritual composting.

When everything is falling apart, you get to choose:

Will I grip harder to what was?

Or will I gather what's true, and build from that?

This doesn't mean you're grateful your life imploded.
It means you're wise enough to sift through the ashes for the gold.

Because let's be honest:

Some things didn't break your heart — they broke your illusion.

Some relationships didn't fall apart — they revealed the imbalance.

Some plans didn't fail — they got out of the way.

The formula for alchemy is simple, but not easy:

Presence + Pattern Recognition + Permission = Growth

Let's break that down:

Presence

You've already practiced this.
You're here. In the now. Not running from it.
Even if your mascara is running and you're holding a half-eaten bucket of Auntie Anne's pretzels from the mall.
(Surviving the storm with cinnamon sugar flakes in your hair and absolutely no shame.)

Pattern Recognition

You're not just watching storms anymore — you're tracking them.
You're seeing how old responses show up.
You're catching the emotional weather patterns before they sweep you away.

(Shoutout to Dorothy — she's still flying, and the data's rolling in.

And RIP Jonas and Eddie… we appreciate your sacrifice,
but dammit, why didn't you just listen?
We told you to hold back — it was shifting!!!)

Because sometimes surviving isn't about outrunning the storm.
It's about reading the sky better next time.
It's about trusting your instincts when everything says go but
your soul says wait.
It's about building a better way forward, not muscling through
broken weather maps.

You're not just watching storms anymore — you're tracking
them.
You're seeing how old responses show up.
You're catching the emotional weather patterns before they
sweep you.

Permission

This is the big one.
Permission to shift.
To respond differently.
To become someone new.

Even if it's clumsy.
Even if you don't have it all figured out.
Even if the people around you preferred the version of you who
didn't ask questions.

Chaos is your permission slip to evolve.

You're not just surviving storms anymore.
You're studying them.
You're listening.

You're planting things in the broken ground.
And you're realizing…

Maybe the breakdown wasn't the end.
Maybe it was the beginning of a better design.

Maybe it was awareness —
the first flicker of seeing what never truly fit.

Maybe it was clarity —
the messy, beautiful unveiling of what you do prefer.
Of what you're ready to build.
Of what you actually want this life to feel like.

Because every storm clears space.

Every ending makes room for a new blueprint.

And you?

You're not stuck in the wreckage.
You're standing at the drawing board.

Chaos didn't break you.
It broke the illusion that you were ever supposed to settle.

"He strolls up to the twister, and he says, 'Have a drink.'
And he chucks the bottle into the twister…
and it never hits the ground."
— Dusty, Twister (1996)

You don't need a plan to be safe.
You need a center.

You are the grounded one now.
The calm in the storm.
The eye in your own chaos.

So be like Bill.
Chuck the bottle into the chaos.
Tell the storm to have a drink.
Because you're not getting sucked in.

CHAPTER 6

Building the New World: Together, Brick by Soulful Brick

"The old world told you to earn your worth.
The new world asks you to embody it."

So here you are —
not in the rubble,
but at the edge of what comes next.

You've made peace with the storm.
You've let the tower fall.
You've remembered your truth.
Now it's time to create a world that matches it.

But here's the thing:

You don't need to rebuild the old house.
You get to build a new home —
one that fits your soul, not you're conditioning.

And this time?
You don't have to do it alone.

This isn't about manifesting a Pinterest board life.

This is about asking:

What kind of life do I want to live from the inside out?

What systems do I never want to recreate?

What rhythms do I want to honor in my daily existence?

And who am I building with — and for?

Because the Phoenix doesn't rise for aesthetics.

It rises to create a life so true
it burns away anything that tries to lie again.

Values as Blueprints

If you've been trained by the old world,
your first instinct might be to say:
"Okay, what should I build? What should I do?"

But if you start building from panic, pressure, or proving —
you'll just recreate another cage.

You don't need a checklist right now.
You need a compass.

Because buildings crumble.
Plans change.
Markets crash.
Relationships evolve.
Trends die.

But values?

Real soul values outlive the storm.
They survive every season.
They become the gravity that holds your world together when
everything else shifts.

So first, we lay the blueprints:

Before you build anything —you get clear on what you're actually building it for.

Ask yourself:

What do I want to feel at the center of my life?

What do I want to always come home to — no matter what happens externally?

What rhythms make me feel like myself?

What is so important to me, I would rebuild it a thousand times if I had to?

Soul Blueprint Examples:

Your blueprint might sound like:

Peace over hustle.
(If it costs me peace, it's too expensive.)

Creativity over conformity.
(My life is my art, not my product.)

Connection over image.
(Real relationships over curated performances.)

Presence over perfection.
(I live where my feet are, not in a someday fantasy.)

Freedom over validation.
(I am not here to earn my belonging.)

Soul Stamp:

You're not here to build a life that impresses strangers.
You're here to build a life that feels like a homecoming to yourself.

To remember the version of you who danced because it felt good.
Who laughed loudly, unapologetically.
Who sang off-key — or on — without worrying if it was "good enough."

The version of you who lived in the present, not the performance.

The one who existed before the world got ahold of you —
before the systems, the pressures, the smallness —
and little by little, dimmed your light.

You are not building to please.
You are not building to perform.
You are building to belong to yourself again.

And every brick you lay in this new life
will be a return to that light.
Brighter.
Fuller.
Free.

It's about remembering the you who was whole before the world demanded edits.

Soulful Community: Why You're Not Meant to Build Alone

Here's the thing:

Healing taught you how to walk alone.
Building will teach you how to walk together again.

You needed that solo season.
The one where you remembered who you are without the noise.
Where you heard your own voice again after years of living on mute.

But now?

Now you're not just surviving.
Now you're creating.
And creation was never meant to be a one-person sport.

What Soulful Community Isn't:

It's not a fan club.

It's not an audience waiting to clap at your performances.

It's not "networking" so you can "collaborate" but secretly just exhaust each other.

What Soulful Community Is:

It's a place where you can show up messy and still be honored.

It's where someone says, "I see you," even when you can't see yourself clearly yet.

It's where you can lay your bricks next to someone else's — not competing, just co-creating.

It's where being honest is more valuable than being impressive.

Because in the New World we're building?

Vulnerability is currency.
Honesty is wealth.
Presence is the power move.

How to Recognize Your Soul Crew:

They leave you feeling full, not drained.

You don't have to over-explain your heart to them.

You're not "too much" for them — you're finally just enough.

They're builders too — not spectators, not critics, not thieves of your light.

Soul Stamp:

Find the ones who make you feel less like you have to be "good enough" and more like you already are.

You don't have to carry every brick alone anymore.
You just have to carry your piece — and trust that others are carrying theirs too.

And together?
We're building cathedrals of freedom out of the rubble they said would bury us.

You've remembered who you are.
You've found the beginnings of your crew.
You're starting to gather the ones who don't just tolerate your light — they celebrate it.

And now?

Now it's time to build.

I promise — it'll be cheaper than that special edition Millennium Falcon LEGO set.
(I mean... have you seen the price on that thing?
More than 10,000 tiny pieces and it still won't even fly. No thank you.)

Because guess what?

We're not building with overpriced plastic.
We're building with the bricks you've been carrying all along.

Every hard-earned lesson.
Every heartbreak.
Every survival skill turned soul skill.
Every heavy thing that made you who you are.

You already have everything you need.

Let's BUILD a life that is vibrationally, unapologetically, exquisitely YOURS.

Vision-Centered Living: Leading with Purpose, Not Performance

In the old world, you lived by survival.
By expectation.
By shoulds and shame and "what will they think?"

But here?
In the New World you're building?

You live by vision.

You lead with purpose,
not pressure.
Desire,
not desperation.
Alignment,
not approval.

Because here's the thing:

If you don't choose the vision, the world will hand you a script —
and call it a life.

And you already know what that felt like.
It almost killed the real you.

Building a Vision-Centered Life Means:

You ask: What do I want my days to feel like?

You move toward what energizes you, not what anesthetizes you.

You recognize that tiny, soul-aligned choices every day build the architecture of joy.

Quick Vision Check:

When you dream now, don't just think:

"What job title will I have?"

"How much money will I make?"

Think:

What will my mornings feel like?

What kind of conversations will fill my days?

What will my body feel like walking through the world?

What energies will be welcome in my space — and which ones won't even get past the threshold?

What will it feel like to belong to my life so fully, I stop chasing escape routes?

Vision Work Isn't "Manifesting Harder."

It's remembering:
You are the architect now.

Every brick you lay — every choice, every boundary, every moment of inspired action —
builds the reality your soul actually came here to live.

And you're not building a shrine to your past anymore.
You're not building a monument to your wounds.
You're building a living cathedral to your becoming.

Final Soul Stamp for Vision-Centered Living:

Your life isn't a product.
It's a frequency.
And you are the one tuning the signal.

You're not rebuilding the old life you outgrew.
You're not patching up the ruins with cheap hope and duct tape.
You're not dragging your wounds into the new world like unpaid baggage handlers.

You're building something different.

You're building a life that feels like freedom in your bones.

You're building with bricks you earned —
and you're laying them down without apology.

You're standing at the crossroads of all the versions of you that were once afraid —
and choosing to fly anyway.

This is the moment when the old gravity loses its grip on you.

This is the moment when you don't ask permission anymore.

This is the moment when you finally say:

"IIIIIIIIIIIIIIIIIIIIT'S
MEEEEEEEEEEEEEEEEEEEEEEEEEEEEEEEEEEEEEEE
EEEEEEEE!"

Wild.
Brilliant.
Unruly.
True.
Fully, radiantly, unapologetically YOU.

You were never here to be small enough to survive the old world.
You are here to be limitless enough to build the new one.

starts singing
"Unliiiiiiiiimiiiiited...
My future is unlimited...
And I've just had a vision, almost like a prophecy..."

The music swells.

The light shifts.

You're floating now.
Lifting.
Becoming.

The old gravity is gone.
The smallness is gone.

Only vision remains.
Only truth remains.
Only the future you were born to create remains.

And it's waiting for you to step in — fully, freely, gloriously.

Epilogue: The Glorious Mess You Stayed For

Let's recap, shall we?

You've mourned Captain Bobby Nash of the 118

You got motivationally screamed at by Col. Jessup before his court-martial.

You let Bruce Nolan speak your inner chaos live from Niagara Falls.

You found peace with Nate the Hoof Guy and Spencer the S&B sorcerer of driveways.

You injected fear with the highest dose of Mounjaro known to the energetic realm.

You faced down an F5 tornado with only a belt, some deep pipes, and a defiant middle finger.

You made a briefcase handoff like you were in Inception.

You ate the full Works Pretzel with Michael Scott.

You danced in the Pink Pony Club like no one was watching and everyone should've been.

You laid your bricks with reverence.

And then?

You soared into Oz like a neon-lit goddess in full voice screaming:

IIIIIIIT'S MEEEEEEEEEEEEEEEEE!

And now you're here.

Still standing.

Still burning.

Still rising.

You, my friend, are the Grinch at the end of the story —
your heart grew three sizes today.

Not because someone handed you the answers.
Not because everything got easy.
But because through chaos, laughter, tears, breakdowns, and
breakthroughs...

You remembered there's a future worth building.
Our future. Together.

How do we end this story?

Maybe Bender throws a fist in the air and Breakfast Clubs us all.
Maybe Doc Brown fires up the DeLorean and shouts, "Where
we're going, we don't need roads."
Maybe Cynthia Erivo gives you a midair nod and whispers, "Told
you."

Maybe Neo shows up with the red pill and says,
"You ready to see how deep this rabbit hole goes?"

And you?
You take it without hesitation.

Because baby...
we're WOKE now.

Not the weird, weaponized version of "woke" that got hijacked
by political chaos.
But the a-WOKE-ning that shakes your soul free.

The kind that says:

"I see it now.
I feel it.
I know who I am.
I know what I came to do.
And I'm not going back to sleep."

You made it through the chaos.
You kept showing up — mascara running, pretzel in hand, bricks
in your backpack.
You laid them down.
You built something true.
And now?

You are the fire.

The light.

The wild, brilliant, hilarious, unstoppable force of a soul
that remembered itself in the middle of the mess —
and rose anyway.

So, cue the montage.
Cue Doctor Strange spinning his rings wide open —
portals appearing across the field, one by one.
Every soul you've ever loved, healed beside, or called your people
—

they step through, ready.

Cue the Wakandan battle cry:
"YIBAMBE!"
("Hold fast." And you will.)

Cue Tony Stark — standing steady, unshakable —
"I am Iron Man."

Because this is the moment you realize...

You're not just rising for yourself.
You're rising with everyone who thought they were too broken, too late, too
tired.

Cue the wind machine.
Cue the "Defying Gravity" encore.
Cue the light that glows brighter every time you whisper...

"It's me."

Cue the final track.
Usher walks in, drenched in metaphorical rain.
The chorus swells.
You, in slow motion, look at everything you just let go of and
whisper back:

"Let it burn."

And then you dance.
Because you can.
Because it's done.
Because you are just getting started.

The Phoenix has risen.
And this time…
she's not coming back down.

You're the flame now.

This isn't the end of your story.
It's the moment you finally picked up the pen.

Now go build it —
the world, the life, the future.

We'll meet you at the portal. (Miss Minutes will make sure we protect the sacred timeline).

Phoenix Flight Plan

A Practical Re-entry Guide for the Wildly Awake

You rose from the ashes. Now here's how to **live the glow**—not just feel it for a chapter.

These aren't goals. They're **reminders. Rituals. Micro-rebellions.**
Let them guide you back to yourself, one unshakable moment at a time.

✈ Daily Soul Practices

- Say **"no"** without guilt once this week.
- Let yourself rest **before** you burn out.
- Dance in your kitchen like no one's watching—and if they are? **Good.**
- Eat the cookie. **Without explaining it to anyone.**
- Take a walk without a destination—**or a podcast.**
- Unfollow one account that makes you forget how powerful you are.
- Say yes to joy **even when nothing's "done."**

✖ Emergency Re-Calibration

- Hand over the guilt. Reclaim the **damn nap.**
- Ground yourself with 3 breaths and a hand over your heart.
- Whisper: *"I belong to myself."* Mean it.
- Call in laughter like it's your *first aid kit.*

- Create. Scribble. Sing. Build. It doesn't have to be useful—just true.

🌱 Reminder for the Road

You are not here to *fix* the old world.
You are here to build the new one—with glitter, grief, joy, and power.

Let every tiny act of alignment be your way of saying:
I didn't just rise. I *arrived*.

(Cue credits. Cue slow fade to gold. Cue wild applause and a standing ovation from the spirit realm.)

✦ You're Still Here?

The credits rolled.
The Phoenix rose.
We dropped mics.
We burned it down, built something better, ate the damn pretzel with ALL the toppings.

And yet… you're still here.
Still curious.
Still craving.
Still secretly wondering:

"Okay, but how do I really live this every day?"

Ohhh, you thought this was just a book?

Nah, babe.
This was just the origin story.

What comes next?

✦ *The workbook.*

♛ *The uprising of wild, radiant souls who stopped asking for permission.*

▥ *The building of something real.*

◐ COMING SOON: The Phoenix Workbook

A Soul Reclamation Journal for the Wildly Ready

You didn't just read a book.
You **remembered** who you are.

Now it's time to **live it**—daily, boldly, imperfectly.

The *Phoenix Workbook* is where that happens.
Inside, you'll find:

✦ Shadow work prompts that don't require sage or shame

✦ Journal questions that feel more like portals than homework

✦ Meditative check-ins to recalibrate when life tries to suck you back in

✦ Space to unravel, rewrite, and reclaim your story— your way

✦ Soul stretches. Truth igniters. Vision blueprints. All of it.

This isn't a place for perfection.
It's a sacred fire pit to **burn what no longer belongs—and build what does.**

You burned it down.
Now let's build something better.

➡ Stay tuned for future workbooks.